HOW-TO OPTIMIZE YOUR WEB STORE
TO MAXIMIZE SALES

 **TUNEUP**

60 WEB STORE TIPS
YOU CAN IMPLEMENT AND USE RIGHT NOW

LUIS A. HERNANDEZ, JR.

Copyright © 2014 by Luis A. Hernandez, Jr.

All rights reserved. No part of this book may be reproduced in any manner whatsoever without written permission, except for brief quotations in articles or reviews.

DISCLAIMER

This publication provides general information about the subject matter. However, the web and ecommerce are dynamic platforms and constantly changing, so neither author nor publisher assumes responsibility, nor do they represent that the information presented is current, valid, true, or appropriate. It is the reader's responsibility to consult with his or her advisors before using any of the ideas or suggestions presented in this work.

This book is the result of the author's experience and opinion, and views expressed are the author's alone and should not be taken as expert instruction. The author and publisher, therefore, specifically disclaim any liability resulting from the application of any of the ideas presented in this book. The information is not intended to serve as professional advice relating to specific situations.

ISBN-13: 978-1494821524
ISBN-10: 1494821524

INTRODUCTION

Many web retailers believe that attracting huge amounts of traffic is the purpose of their web stores.

Well, I have news for you.

The purpose of a store, whether online or bricks-and-mortar, is to sell stuff and make a profit.

That's it!

Nothing happens until you sell something.

Web traffic and visitors are important, of course, but are you doing enough to sell merchandise to current prospects?

If you are focusing exclusively on generating tons of traffic and thinking that large numbers of people will be the solution, you may end up being disappointed.

Concentrate instead on ensuring web site visitors who take the time to explore your web store are able to find what they are seeking, and then complete the transaction in the least amount of time.

The purpose of **ADD to CART TUNEUP** is to help you – the ecommerce site owner – present your products properly so you can turn existing store visitors into paying customers.

Once you achieve that goal, you then can concentrate on attracting more web traffic.

If you can master the art of making it easy and pleasant for customers to buy from you, your success as a web retailer is closer at hand.

I hope this book will serve as a helpful guide to your destination.

And just like the thinking that inspired it, I've purposely kept **ADD-TO-CART TUNEUP** brief and to the point.

I imagine you are busy with your website and would like the "nuts and bolts" on what you can do to sell more, NOW, so there is no need for fluff or distracting text.

Less is more.

That should be your mantra.

Luis Hernandez, Jr.

Orange City, Florida
January 2014

1 | Make Pages Easy to Read

Let me give you two examples of the same paragraph. You tell me which one is easier on the eyes and brain.

Example 1

> Two roads diverged in a yellow wood, and sorry I could not travel both, and be one traveler, long I stood, and looked down one as far as I could, to where it bent in the undergrowth. Then took the other, as just as fair, and having perhaps the better claim, because it was grassy and wanted wear, though as for that the passing there, had worn them really about the same.

Example 2

> Two roads diverged in a yellow wood,
>
> And sorry I could not travel both
>
> And be one traveler, long I stood
>
> And looked down one as far as I could
>
> To where it bent in the undergrowth.
>
> Then took the other, as just as fair,
>
> And having perhaps the better claim
>
> Because it was grassy and wanted wear,
>
> Though as for that the passing there
>
> Had worn them really about the same.

Had Robert Frost used the first approach, I don't think *The Road Less Taken* would've become as popular as it was destined to be. Well, at least not online.

Reading anything online takes a little more effort than reading the same text on paper. Therefore, it puts additional strain on the eyes, which means we tend to read more slowly when staring at a screen.

This also means we easily can be distracted, because reading online takes more determination.

Therefore, make paragraphs shorter and content easy to grasp, and use ample spacing between text lines.

People don't read online.

They scan.

2 | Use Plain Fonts

Again, this has to do with readability.

If I was to use this beautiful font in an attempt to get my message across I'd probably lose you sooner rather than later.

As an old newspaper guy once told me, "When in doubt, use Helvetica."

The gist of the message is to keep it simple and consistent.

Whether you decide to use Verdana, Tahoma, Georgia, or any other easy-to-read font designed specifically for the web, heed the spirit of that advice.

3 | Use Big Fonts

Now that I mentioned "readability," it's only fair to ensure that those clean, simple fonts you plan to use will be visible.

If this is the equivalent of a size 10 font, you tell me if you think the average person will be comfortable reading this short sentence.

Now, for comparison purposes, this is the equivalent of a size 14 font.
Tell me which one is easier to read.

Let's not forget that computer monitors render images and text as a series of dots.

Smaller text will be harder to read, especially for older people, so your site demographics should be taken into account.

Don't make customers strain their eyes when they read product descriptions.

4 | Create a Great Logo

Spend a few bucks to make your "brand" stand out. There are hundreds (maybe thousands) of affordable web services that will create a great logo for your business in a short time and for a reasonable fee.

Many will give you several options from which to choose, while others will present ideas from dozens of artists, allowing you to select the one you think works better for your business.

Having a great-looking logo is a small investment that can make a huge difference.

Choose to look professional.

Below are just a few logo design services to give you an idea of what's available and what they offer:

http://99designs.com/logo-design

http://www.logomaker.com/watch-it-work.html

http://www.logoarena.com/

http://www.crowdspring.com/

You can also find qualified logo designers through Elance.com.
https://www.elance.com/logo-designers-jobs/77

5 | Use Big Brand Names to Your Benefit

If you use the services of big companies such as FedEx®, UPS®, or the United States Postal Service®, for example, use their logos.

If you accept credit cards such as Visa®, MasterCard®, American Express®, and Discover®, or an online service such as PayPal®, use their logos.

Your business is rated A+ by the Better Business Bureau? Download its official artwork to use.

Show your customers with whom you do business.

BONUS TIP

If you are not a member of the Better Business Bureau, you may want to look into becoming one.

Contact the BBB office nearest you for more details.

Additionally, listing any other professional associations of which you are a member may also be a good idea.

6 | Use Social Media

If you have a Facebook® and Google+® account, for example (and you should), link to it from your web store.

But, don't create a social media page only to prove that you lack social graces.

The best use of social media is to talk about your customers ... in a nice way, of course.

In other words, don't use it to advertise or promote what you are selling. Rather, use it to showcase those who use your products or services.

If you sell car parts, for example, don't use it to run ads about stuff you are selling.

Boring!

Instead, showcase customers who have purchased from you and who are using those items.

People love to see their pictures "in print," and will also help promote your site by sharing those types of posts, which are far more fun than advertisements disguised as news.

7 | Use Fewer Words

I mentioned earlier that people scan; they don't read online. If you can get your message across by using half the number of words than originally planned, then do so.

Keep editing for brevity.

Write your product description then walk away for a few minutes. When you go back, try to convey the same message with less text.

Don't use unnecessary words; especially "buzz words" or "industry" jargon.

Let your competition sound silly.

Stick to basics and don't use a lot of words to get your message across.

A good idea is to ask a friend or an industry outsider to proof your copy.

Don't be surprised when you hear "What does this word mean?" If you do, replace that word immediately with one everyone can understand.

8 | Check Your Spelling and Grammar

In this day and age, typos and other grammatical errors are easy to avoid.

Having product descriptions full of typos or bad grammar is unnecessary and reflects badly on your site.

Take the improper use of apostrophes, for example.
The apostrophe has to be the most frequently misused punctuation mark.

There are many computer-based programs, as well as online services — many of them free — that will check both the spelling and the grammar of your product descriptions, so make it a habit to take advantage of them.

Many prospects may be turned off by copy errors, stop right there, and go elsewhere to make a purchase, especially if the product description is of a technical nature.

9 | Use a Menu Bar

Every page on your store should have a menu bar on the left hand side of the page. Alternatively, you can have the menu bar running horizontally, right under the page header.

Why that location?

Because most big ecommerce websites place their menu bars in either location. That's why.

Make the menu easy to read and understand, but don't make it so big or long as to render it unusable.

If necessary, have a "fly out" menu that is visible, uncluttered, and easy-to-use.

Have your menu categorized logically, so website visitors know exactly which section they need to visit to locate the items they want.

Think of a restaurant menu. It gives you a quick general view of food items available, grouped in related categories.

10 | Sitemaps

Sitemaps can be confusing to many e-merchants, and proof of that are the HTML sitemaps you find in many sites.

For the most part, as far as providing helpful navigation to the average site visitor, they are useless.

To search engines they may look like spammy pages, based on the number of links. Therefore, if your store carries hundreds or thousands of items, your sitemap may be hurting you.

Instead, if you must have a sitemap for your human visitors, then design it for them. Make it practical and easy-to-use, so they can find whatever they may be seeking.

On the other hand, if your site offers good search capabilities, then the site map hardly will be used, although it may still serve a purpose to some.

What about search engines?

Yes, you want to provide a sitemap to them, but for it to be effective, it must be in XML format.

For more information about Sitemaps, visit:

https://support.google.com/webmasters/answer/156184

Your ecommerce provider, most likely, is already taking care of making an XML sitemap of your site to search engines. But if you need to generate one, have someone who's well versed on this subject give you advice in this area.

11 | Provide a "Homepage" Link

Whether you use your company logo for this purpose, or you use a text link, every page on your site should have an easy-to-find link that takes visitors back to your homepage with one click.

Traditionally, this link is located in the header of the page, and positioned on the left side, right above the menu bar.

Don't reinvent the wheel when it comes to this.

Add a homepage link if your store lacks one.

12 | Provide Site Search

I'd say that at least 90% of people who use the Internet for fun or work are conditioned to search, so most prospects who arrive at your site via the homepage, will automatically look for a search field.

Therefore, it is crucial for you to make such a feature available on your site.

If you already offer site search, then be certain it easily is accessible and visible.

From my own experience I can tell you that customers who use internal site search are more likely to complete their purchase than those that do not.

Make your site's search field prominent.

13 | Provide Targeted Searches

Let's say that you offer clothing for children and adults, both male and female. Then, a man searching for pants would benefit greatly from eliminating all kid's and women's pants from the search results he sees.

Giving the customer control, as far as refining searches for results that only relate to his interests, is very important.

For example, if I am searching for parts for a 1989 Pontiac Trans Am and I am shown a list of parts that fit a 1979 Pontiac Trans Am, they would be of no use to me.

As a potential customer, I want you to show me stuff I can use. The rest is nothing more than background noise.

Keep those types of scenarios in mind when designing and incorporating search parameters for your store.

Make your internal site search useful in order to prevent prospects from going back to the search engine that brought them to your site in the first place. That's a bad signal and, by then, you might have lost them forever.

14 | Use Bullet Points

Going back to the "Scanning vs. Reading" scenario, bullet points make the scanning part a lot faster and easier.

For example:

This is a shopping list that includes Matches, Aluminum Foil, Milk, Soda, Sugar, Flour, Rice, Chocolate, and Water.

And this is the same list presented as bullet points:

- Matches
- Aluminum Foil
- Milk
- Soda
- Sugar
- Flour
- Rice
- Chocolate
- Water

Whenever possible, use bulleted lists for highlighting item features, benefits, etc.

Alternatively, a numbered list may be appropriate in certain cases, but both serve the same purpose.

Create "hot spots" to keep prospects engaged.

15 | Allow Customers to Contact You

I consider it almost a requirement to see a mailing address as well as a phone number every time I consider doing business with smaller companies.

If I see no easy way of contacting them should a problem arise, I usually take my business elsewhere.

Make it easy for your customers to see where you are located, and give them a physical address, not only a P.O Box.

Also, give them a contact phone number.

In this day and age of cell phones, I don't consider the "toll-free" number as important as it used to be, but if you have one, make it easy to find, and offer both the toll-free number as well as your regular phone, for local customers and people who may be outside the United States.

Needless to say, your customer service email address should be visible on every single page of your site.

16 | Copyright Notices

They may not be important as far as helping you complete a sale, but I've seen many out-of-date Copyright Notices that make you wonder if the company is still in business.

So, if you feel you need to have a Copyright Notice on yours, at least make sure you update it every year in order to keep it current.

In my opinion, they are nothing more than a waste of bandwidth because if someone wants to copy your contents, chances are you'll never know (or will find out too late), and you are protected whether you post a copyright notice or not.

But, again, if you must have one, make sure it is up to date.

17 | Privacy

Your customers deserve to know what you are doing to protect their privacy, and how you intend to use the information they provide.

You need to have a "Privacy" page that addresses those concerns clearly and accurately.

On this page you should explain what happens during and after they share their info with you, and you will have happier customers.

Keep it simple and free of legal mumbo jumbo.

Having a Privacy Policy page also may be a good signal to search engines, so make sure to make one available.

18 | Website Security

Just like by addressing Privacy concerns, your site will benefit by having a page that explains, in simple language, what measures you have in place that make your web store safe for entering financial information, such as credit cards.

This page is also the place to talk about checkout pages, shopping cart security, SSL certification, and data encryption.

Display security third-party logos and links to certificates.

You must prove to customers that it is safe for them to conduct business with you.

19 | Money-Back Guarantee

Offering a Money-Back Guarantee highlights the fact that you stand behind customers by letting them know that you will take their purchase back if they are not satisfied with it.

Regardless of how great your photos or product descriptions may be, your customers will not be able to touch what they are buying. Therefore, you are asking them to trust you.

Trust is a two-way street.

Offer a money-back guarantee.

20 | Shipping Information

This one can make or break your business.
No two ways about it.

Customers want what they ordered today, delivered tomorrow, as impossible, unreasonable, or expensive as that may be. You need to have a clear explanation about how fast you will get the stuff they've just purchased into their hands.

Make this page brief and crystal-clear as to what they can expect.

If you do not ship on weekends, say so.

If what they ordered needs to be manufactured, you have to explain that, and also give them an accurate estimate as to when it will be shipped.

In summary, make sure customers know and understand:

1. The date when you will ship the goods

2. Which carrier will deliver them

3. And, if available, tracking information they will receive when the item is on its way

21 | Terms of Use

The small print, as it's usually called, is a good idea for most sites. Again, all you need is a simple page with a list of terms and conditions of web site use.

For example:

- Who owns the graphics used on your site
- Detailed Copyright information
- Electronic communication details
- Who owns the site content
- How feedback/comments will be used
- Ownership of trademarks and brands used
- Linking rules
- Arbitration in case of disputes

And more.

Again, not a bad idea to consider as it helps your site look professional. You may want to talk to your attorney in order to draft your own Terms and Conditions page.

22 | Floating Cart

I believe that most ecommerce/shopping cart providers are making this feature available to their users.

A floating shopping cart keeps track of either the number of items that a customer has placed in his/her shopping cart (by clicking the "Add to Cart" button), a running total of the current items in the cart, or both.

A "Go to Checkout" or similar link or button takes the customer to the checkout page, where the purchase may be completed.

If your provider or developer can make this feature available to you, use it.

Keep your customers informed during every step of their visit to your store.

23 | Product Photos

Take good, sharp photos of the items you sell. In this day and age of relatively inexpensive digital cameras, there is no excuse for having bad pictures on your site.

If appropriate, make bigger photos available for customers to view. Ideally these would be embedded in a "Light Table," but regardless of format, they usually are a good idea, especially where item details are important for closing a sale.

Use lots of photos if the product demands it.

Close ups can be important in some cases, so make those available. Different angles may be another thing to consider. And if you need to show size, a photo of a ruler next to the item may give the customer an idea of scale.

I am sure that when you purchase items online you like to see lots of pics. I know I do. Every time I buy something on eBay, for example, good photos make a big difference.

Think like a customer.

BONUS TIP

If photos are crucial for you to make a sale, especially where close-ups and high detail is concerned, you may want to invest money in a professional camera, and maybe even a portable light studio or tent, in order to have good control of lighting, reflections, shadows, etc.

24 | Sale Prices

They should be visible and large enough to get people's attention.

Having a bold, visible sale price is key, as well as a sign of your confidence that your price is better than that of your competitors.

$24.95

is not as effective as

$24.95

when vying for attention.

25 | Free Shipping

There is no doubt that Free Shipping is what every customer wants, even though there's no such thing. Someone has to pay for items to get delivered.

But if that's what they want, why not offer it to them?

Having a Free Shipping option does not necessarily mean that you have to absorb that cost.

Free shipping is about perception.

If, for example, you sell item **A** for $24.95 plus shipping, and the average shipping cost adds up to $3.95, then experiment with offering item **A** for $28.90 Free Shipping (US 48), for example.

Notice that the Free Shipping scenario shown above is for deliveries *only* within the contiguous 48 states, which is the only formula I know works well.

You can also set a pre-determined dollar amount that triggers the Free Shipping option; just don't make it too high.

Free Shipping takes the "thinking" away, and that simplifies the "purchase it now" decision.

26 | Whole Numbers

Restaurants are notorious for using this technique, and it may be something with which you can experiment.

Even though $23.95 is a nickel cheaper than $24, $23.95 "appears" to be a larger number because of the decimal point and the 95 cents, while $24 looks smaller.

This technique may work well, especially when combined with Free Shipping.

I believe most people prefer whole amounts when shopping.

27 | MSRP

The MSRP, or Manufacturer's Suggested Retail Price, is nothing more than a suggestion, and unless your supplier has a Minimum Advertised Price (MAP) pricing policy in place, it is very likely that your competitors are selling the same merchandise below MSRP.

If you will offer a discount off MSRP, it is a good idea to list the MSRP in regular text and with a strike-through to show you are "slashing" the suggested retail price.

For example:

MSRP $~~29.95~~

YOU PAY ONLY **$25**

BONUS TIP

You may also want to include a "you save" line to show how much money the customer is saving. I do not think that using a percentage is as effective, compared to actual dollar amount savings.

28 | Add to Cart

Arguments as well as studies have been conducted about whether an "Add to Cart" button is more effective than one that reads "Buy it Now." I consider it a silly argument.

If I am ready to make a purchase I don't care what the button says, as long as I am able to complete my purchase.

But semantics aside, make sure that the "Add to Cart" button (or whatever you choose to call it), is large, visible, and easy to find. And I don't care if it's red, yellow, green, or blue.

Yes, additional "studies" indicate that red may not be as effective as green because our brains interpret the color red as an emergency signal, a sign to stop, and all that nonsense.

Anyway, you decide which color works best for you. Just make sure it stands out! And post the estimated shipping date right next to the "Add to Cart" button.

A short line of small text is all that's required.

 SHIPS NEXT BUSINESS DAY

BONUS TIP

Stand about 3 to 4 feet away from your monitor while looking at one of your product pages.

If you are unable to easily spot the "Add to Cart" button, make it larger or brighter.

#29 | Inventory Availability

Customers not only want cheap prices, no sales tax, and free shipping, they also want their purchases delivered fast.

If you want to succeed in ecommerce, you have to ship merchandise as quickly as possible. Therefore, if you must rely on a 3rd party to do the shipping for you, you have to make certain they will fulfill your orders promptly.

Backorders can be the "kiss of death" for a business.

But, because we live in an imperfect world, backorders are a fact of life. So how you deal with backorders is the key.

If there's a way for you to display an "In Stock" notice based on current inventory levels, that's a great way to help make sales. Quantities may not be as important, but again, if your site allows you dynamically to display quantities in stock, consider doing so.

However, if customers can place an order regardless of items being in stock (*over-ordering*), you must let them know as soon as possible that there will be a delay.

Be proactive. Do not wait until the customer calls to inquire about their order to deliver the bad news. If you do, more than likely you will be issuing a refund.

People tend to be understandable when they realize that someone is doing their best to take care of them, so "bite the bullet" and deal with the unpleasant as promptly as you can.

It may help you save a sale.

30 | Returns Policy

This is not a matter of *if,* but rather *when.*

Someone, at some point, will want to return what they've just purchased, so make sure that near the "Add to Cart" button you provide a link to how you handle returns.

Similar to large photos, a light-box or pop-up window is the best way to handle this task.

Return rules are best if kept simple and to the point. If you offer 30 days, say so. Who pays shipping for returns must be clear. If there will be a restocking fee, explain that part.

Keep it brief, simple, and professional, so it does not keep customers from completing their purchase.

And you may also want to include an "Exchange" offer, if appropriate, because this can engender trust and also save a sale.

A returns policy should be in place and easily accessible to give customers peace of mind.

31 | Social Media Distractions

Your customer is thinking about buying an item from your store, and right next to the "Add to Cart" button you have a bunch of icons advertising Facebook®, Pinterest®, Google+®, "email your friends," and more.

Why?

In my opinion this is nothing more than a distraction, as useful and fun as those services are.

If you must have them, I don't have a problem with that as long as you show them AFTER the transaction is complete.

Let your customers go through the checkout process without distractions, and allow them to broadcast to the world about their purchase *after* the purchase is complete, not before.

There is a place and time for those distractions.

The "Add to Cart" section is not that place or time.

32 | Landing Pages

Every page of your site is a landing page.

I am not clear why some merchants think that the "home" page is the only one that can be referred to as the landing page.

Customers will arrive at your site through any available page. Ergo, every page is as important as the homepage and should be treated accordingly.

If a search engine is pointing to a product or items page, that's where customers will land. And that's why it's crucial to have good titles and product descriptions, in addition to good internal navigation.

You want to make sure customers stay on your site instead of "bouncing back" to the search engine.

A high bounce rate is a very bad signal to search engines, as well as a chance of losing a potential customer forever.

A bounce rate of 50% or more is a reason for concern. A rate of 75% and higher means you have a major problem.

You control the elements and content of every landing page on your site, so make them appealing and engaging and customers will stick around, giving you a better chance of making another sale.

33 | Breadcrumbs

Their purpose is to provide a trail back to your site's homepage from your present location within the website.

Think of it as the "You are here" big red dot you see on store maps at large shopping malls.

Breadcrumb trails should be unobtrusive and dynamically generated for maximum efficiency.

I am not 100% clear if they are mostly beneficial for customer navigation or for search engine purposes, but they can help people find their way within a web store, so they are definitely a must-have for ecommerce sites.

Here's a typical example:

Homepage | Section 1 | Subsection

Breadcrumb trails should be hot linked to each respective category, and located toward the top of the page for easy access.

34 | Page Title

Each page title must be unique.

This means that if your store has 250 pages, you should have 250 unique page titles.

It not only should describe the product on the page exactly and accurately, but it must also be readable to humans. In other words, you are writing for your customers, not search engine bots.

As a page title, it is a good idea to use a larger font to make it stand out.

Example:

My Unique Product Title

This area is reserved for a photo of the product.

ADD to CART

SHIPS NEXT BUSINESS DAY

And this area is for the "Add to Cart" button, item number, etc.

35 | Item or Part Numbers

As the web becomes more organized, it is a good idea to use standardized identifiers for products.

This allows customers to ensure they are getting the item they want, as well as conduct price comparisons, check for availability, etc.

Common identifiers include UPC codes for general products and ISBNs for books, for example.

Of course you can (and should) use your own product numbers for internal control, but it may be a good idea to make provisions also to list industry standard identifiers, such as UPCs or ISBNs as the case may be. This allows your products to be included in additional searches.

Just make sure the data you enter is 100% correct.

36 | Product Description

Product descriptions came under attack by search engines a while back because of the widespread use of what is referred to as duplicate content.

Retailers were using product descriptions provided by the manufacturers verbatim, which although accurate and a time-saver, is something that search engines (especially Google®) frown upon.

So, the best policy is to take the time to create your own and unique product descriptions.

Keep in mind that you are not writing them in order to get awarded a Pulitzer Prize. Simply describe your products to the best of your ability, using words your customers use.

Don't over-complicate the process.

Also, use your company name as part of the description, in case your content gets scraped by other sites.

There is no fool-proof method to prevent others from copying your content, but that should not discourage you from writing good descriptions and making them unique to your site.

You may also want to ask some of your customers to write their thoughts on a particular product they purchased from you in exchange for a discount coupon or something of that nature.

People love to see their name in print, and that may also help you gain more traction through social media sites.

37 | Product Specs

Yes, this is mainly boring, boilerplate stuff, but it can help customers decide on making a purchase by insuring that the product they are looking at is the one they want.

The Product Specs section should be at the very end of the product description and be brief.

This area is ideal for listing info such as ISBN or UPC numbers, manufacturer, and other pertinent details, such as materials used, power requirements, restrictions, and more.

Give customers the item specs, as boring as they may be.

38 | Shopping Cart

Even though the terms "Shopping Cart" and "Checkout" are often used interchangeably, the fact is that they are completely different and should be treated accordingly, at least from your perspective.

The Shopping Cart is where items to be purchased are placed.

Customer-friendly Shopping Carts allow customers clearly to see what it is they are buying, the unit price, quantity, and total cost.

Customers should have the ability to amend the quantity desired and the cart should do all calculations on the fly.

A good idea is to have a "Continue Shopping" link or button if the customer wants to add more items.

If the customer is ready to check out, then a clearly visible button offering to "Continue to Checkout" should be available on the shopping cart page.

39 | Shopping Cart Extras

If shipping and handling charges are not clear before this step, many customers will put items in their cart in order to determine what the shipping charges will be.

This action can result in a high number of abandoned shopping carts, because to get a shipping amount, the customer has to provide more information, such as name, address, etc., in many cases only to be "sticker shocked" due to excessive shipping charges.

To prevent or minimize this occurrence, shopping cart pages are an excellent place to include items that may help customers complete the transaction.

Information such as brief customer testimonials may be all that's required to influence someone to hit "Continue to Checkout."

If you offer shipping discounts or free shipping, this is a great opportunity to mention that fact again.

Reminding the customer that merchandise may be returned within a specific amount of time may help close the sale for some.

Lastly, graphics from the Better Business Bureau®, your SSL security certificate, and others, may give some customers the peace of mind they need in order to shop with confidence and complete the transaction.

40 | Checkout

It may appear silly that we need to tell customers that store checkouts are "secure." Then, again, there still may be a few companies out there doing shady things, so it is a good idea to remind your customers that they are safe doing business with you.

Checkout systems are varied, but I strongly believe that the most effective kind is the single- or one-page checkout.

A single-page checkout is a form that provides fields for Bill-To and Ship-To information, as well as other contact information such as phone number and email address, plus payment methods.

You'll never go wrong helping customers save time and money, and a single-page checkout does just that.

Consider using one for your store.

Keep in mind that if you use shipping and handling charges as a profit center, customers may click away without completing the transaction, so you may need to review this approach.

Use your store analytics data to pinpoint the number of abandoned carts. You cannot fix problems effectively without knowing exactly what those problems may be.

41 | Credit Cards

I believe that you have to make it easy for people to do business with you, and in order to do so you must be willing to accept all credit cards.

Some people argue that American Express® fees, for example, are too high and, therefore, they won't accept Amex® products. That's your right, of course, but I believe you only shortchange yourself by not being flexible.

I much rather make a little less money than lose a sale, but that's just me.

And, I just want to make it clear that I do not work for Amex® or other credit card company, so it does not matter to me which ones you decide to accept.

However, it may make a huge difference to some of your customers.

42 | PayPal®

Not all store systems work with PayPal®, so you will have to check with your provider to see if it offers PayPal implementation.

If it is possible, I encourage you to add PayPal as one of your payment gateways.

It seems to me that more and more people are using PayPal as their online payment service of choice, so you cannot afford to ignore it as a viable channel.

If your provider allows it, accept PayPal.

43 | Checkout Extras

Once a customer has reached the final stages of the checkout page, the commitment to complete the transaction has crossed the tipping point, but you may still want to add a comment or two from satisfied customers.

The sale is not complete until the customer clicks the "Submit Order" button.

But before he/she consummates the transaction, you may be tempted to ask for a few more bits of info. This is dangerous terrain, so tread carefully.

Avoid, at all costs, asking for things that may distract the customer from completing the transaction.

Questions such as how did you hear about us, for instance, might be more suitable during the "thank you for your purchase" phase instead of now.

On the other hand, if the purchase is a gift and/or the customer has special handling and/or delivery instructions, then those fields are perfectly acceptable. Just remember to keep them business-like and to the point.

The sale is not complete, yet.

And speaking of that ... make sure the "Submit Order Now," or whatever you decide to name the call to action, is big, visible, and clear.

At one point I added a "You must click the button to complete your order" comment with an arrow pointing to the button, and that helped increase sales.

Little did we know that those phone calls from customers complaining about not receiving their orders were due to the fact that they had failed to click the "Submit Order" button, as strange as that sounds.

Therefore, make it obvious that customers have to click that final button so their order gets submitted.

44 | "Thank You for Your Purchase" Page

Having such a page tells the customer that the order was successfully submitted and that it is now in your queue, waiting to be processed.

Additionally, you can let the customer know how soon you will get to his or her order, and what your standard shipping procedures entail. Things such as how fast the order gets processed when it is placed on a Saturday night, for example, may prevent calls to your customer service department while the item is in transit.

The "Thank You for Your Purchase" page is also a good place to reiterate your return policies, remind customers to give feedback on their purchase, write a product review, or simply share their purchase with their friends through social media sites.

Provide hot links to make the process easier.

BONUS TIP

Customers like to be valued and appreciated, so design a nice "Thank You" page.

You cannot say "Thank You" too many times.

45 | Order Confirmation Email

Any self-respecting ecommerce provider will offer this feature to its clients. If yours does not, maybe the time has come to consider a different platform.

The confirmation email makes sure the customer knows his/her order went through. This adds peace of mind for them and prevents time wasted answering emails or phone calls from customers wanting to know if you received their order.

Keep the order confirmation email brief and make sure it shows what they ordered, which size and color, if applicable, and also the shipping information they provided.

I have lost count of the number of emails and calls we received after the order had been placed to let us know they had entered the wrong address. It happens, and you want to correct that information *before* the package goes out.

A few links or icons to your Facebook, Google+, and Pinterest page, for example, should be placed at the end of the email.

Avoid the "please like our page" commentary. Your customers know how to "like" pages and all that.

46 | Order Shipped Email

As with the order confirmation email, your service provider should have an automated email system that sends an email when you mark an order as shipped.

And as with the order confirmation email, this one should be brief and have the package tracking information, ideally as a hot link directly to the carrier's tracking detail page.

This email is an excellent opportunity to ask the customer for product feedback after purchase is received.

Use such commentary to augment your product pages with a "Product Feedback" block. This is helpful to your unique content, as well as to help with sales.

Customers love to hear what others have to say about items they are considering buying.

This feedback is also important to you, the seller. If customers dislike a certain product and give it bad reviews, maybe you should think about not offering it.

Also give your customer the option to stop receiving emails from you. Most will be okay with receiving info from you (don't abuse this privilege), but if a few ask to be removed from your email distribution list, do so immediately.

Always respect your customer's wishes.

47 | Page Background Color

Use white or off-white for the background, on every page.

Don't be afraid of white.

Colors, especially dark ones, are a turn off for most people, so don't try to get creative regardless of what your artistic mind may be telling you.

Use white or off-white.

48 | Text Color

Use black or a dark shade of gray for regular text, on every page.

Don't be afraid of black text.

If you start feeling creative, open any book or a newspaper and notice the ink color.

Follow that lead.

Use black or dark gray.

49 | Link Colors

There are three standard colors used on links:

- Standard or body links: Blue ("#0000FF")

- Visited links: Purple ("#800080")

- Active links: Red ("#FF0000")

Don't stray too far (if at all) from this rule.

50 | Music, Sound, and Animations

If it is 100% related to your product, such as a voice or sound recording, a song, music, or anything that uses or requires some form of animation to demonstrate the product, go ahead and make it a part of the product description. But, you must give absolute playback control to the end-user.

Never start any type of playback without user knowledge. Doing so is annoying and old fashioned.

What was cool and acceptable back in 1999, no longer is.

Remember that if it has nothing to do with the product offered, it does not belong on your site.

BONUS TIP

Videos are an excellent tool for you to demonstrate how an item or product works. Just don't use background music, unless it is absolutely necessary.

Keep product demo videos under 1 minute.

51 | Footers

We've all seen page footers that are nothing more than a futile attempt to feed search engine bots.

If you feel you have to resort to those types of tactics, you are missing the point.

Your web store should be optimized for your customers. They are the final authority when it comes to making a purchase.

I was directly involved with ecommerce for more than 15 years, and I can promise you that not a single purchase was ever made by a search engine bot.

Therefore, if your store has a link- and text-laden footer, do some house cleaning and eliminate all that stuff.

The only information that belongs there (or elsewhere on your site), is information that will be helpful to your customers.

Simplify!

52 | Recently-Viewed Items

This is a feature that may help customers make a purchase decision when viewing similar items.

You may have to talk with your store developer to determine if making the feature available is possible.

Usually such links are located on the right-hand column (assuming your store architecture allows for a 3rd column on the right side of the page).

The text link should be the title of the page with an exact description of the item (for easy identification purposes). Sometimes a small image may be used, but this is not absolutely necessary.

The idea behind this is, of course, to allow the customer easily to locate the item they viewed previously, in case they want to view it again.

53 | Related Product Links

These types of links are usually found at the end of the product description, and they are helpful to your customers as well as for optimization reasons.

Having such links may allow you to sell multiple items, something that helps reduce shipping costs.

Related product links are usually text-only links, and they basically indicate that the product recommended is similar to the one being displayed.

This gives more product exposure and it also gives the customer options, something that most customers like and appreciate.

If an image is to be used, something small is all that's necessary; but, again, a text link itself usually suffices.

54 | Order Block Positioning

Without a doubt, the order block (the area that contains the "Add to Cart" button, and all associated information), should appear "above the fold."

Above the fold is an old newspaper expression that describes the newspaper area that's visible when the newspaper is folded in half, resulting on the top portion of the page being visible, while the bottom half remains hidden.

You want your website's name and logo (the header), plus the search field, breadcrumbs trail, the title of the item, a good photo, and the order block to appear "above the fold."

Some of the description may appear also, along with some of the navigation menu on the left side and the recently viewed items on the right side, but the focus should be on the item itself and how to purchase it.

# 55 | Secondary Order Block

Some retailers have experimented with a secondary order block at the very end of the item description, especially when a lot of scrolling down the page hides the "Add to Cart" button.

The jury's still out on whether that's really necessary – or overkill – but the idea is not necessarily a bad one.

In lieu of a secondary order block, you may want to incorporate a "Back to top of page" link or image that automatically brings the main order block back into view, without the need for the customer to scroll back up to it.

Again, it's not clear whether this helps or not, but it cannot hurt, and sometimes experimenting with these "customer conveniences" can yield pleasant results.

56 | Page Width

Your web page should be viewable regardless of the size of the monitor used to browse your site.

Talk to your web developer to insure your site utilizes the most real estate possible without compromising design or usability.

However, one consideration may involve limiting the *minimum* width area, so design elements remain in harmony with the remainder of your website.

But, the most important aspect to consider is never to force your customers to scroll sideways for them to be able to read the page content.

Page width should always be dynamic.

57 | Web Browsers

Don't limit yourself to one browser to determine if your site looks right. Different browsers may render your webpages with slight differences, while some features may not work as intended.

At minimum, use a current version of MS Internet Explorer®, Google Chrome®, and Apple Safari® to look at your site. Put a couple of items in the shopping cart and make sure you can get all the way to the checkout page.

If you notice significant differences and/or errors, report these immediately to your developer.

Errors among browsers will affect some customers who may not be knowledgeable enough to try a different browser in order to have the ability to complete a transaction. Those customers will simply go shopping at your competitor's web store.

Don't allow that to happen!

Make sure your site is fully functional with all the popular web browsers.

58 | Tablets

By all means take the time to see how your website appears when browsed with a tablet PC.

And, just as with different browsers, put it to the test to insure all features are working as intended, and make a test order to see if you can go through the checkout process.

Thousands of people are switching daily from conventional personal computers to tablets, so make sure customers will be able to place orders when they view your store with an iPad® or similar device.

59 | Smart Phones

You should talk to your developer or web provider to have your site converted for it to be easily accessible through mobile phones.

Just because your site can be viewed through a smartphone's web browser does not mean that customers will care for that particular shopping experience.

You have to insure your web store is mobile-friendly in order to make the shopping experience a pleasant one.

Also keep in mind that mobile Internet usage is projected to overtake desktop Internet access by late 2014. So, if your website does not render properly on smartphone screens, this may end up costing you sales.

Don't throw this important to-do item onto the back burner.

BONUS TIP

There are companies that specialize in converting websites into full-featured mobile sites. The process does not take long, but service fees may apply. Do some research before making a decision.

But, don't wait too long.

60 | Focus Groups

You won't need a large room full of cameras and recording equipment, or even a two-way mirror; just a volunteer willing to help in exchange for a few bucks (restaurant or supermarket gift cards are great for this).

Sit him or her in front of your homepage and give a simple assignment:

Find a certain product in your store and purchase it.

No, they don't have to actually buy it, just get as close to completing the transaction short of entering credit card information.

Step back so you can observe "the customer" and the screen.

Do not say a word.

You are not there to coach on how to use your web site. Further, if he or she needs coaching on how to find and purchase an item from your store, that's a red flag and you have to be ready to note the comments down.

Use complete strangers for this experiment. Friends or family members are not ideal candidates.

A thick skin may be required.

In Closing

Quit chasing web traffic thinking that it will be the silver bullet that will propel your sales through the roof.

Focus on serving existing customers to the best of your ability and making sure your store is optimized to convert current visitors into paying customers.

If, by implementing a single tip from this book, you generate just ONE additional sale every other day, your return on investment will be significant.

Take your time to study and adopt a few of the suggestions I make. Some (if not the great majority) will work for you, but make the decision to shake things up a bit and incorporate some changes to the way you do business.

You have lots to gain.

I wish you health, happiness, and prosperity.

Sincerely,

Luis A. Hernandez, Jr.

Visit http://www.carttuneup.com/ and share your thoughts, comments and ideas with me.

I also am on:

LinkedIn http://www.linkedin.com/in/lhernandezjr/

Google+ https://plus.google.com/+LuisHernandezJr/posts

Table of Contents

INTRODUCTION 3

1 | Make Pages Easy to Read 5

2 | Use Plain Fonts 7

3 | Use Big Fonts 8

4 | Create a Great Logo 9

5 | Use Big Brand Names to Your Benefit 10

6 | Use Social Media 11

7 | Use Fewer Words 12

8 | Check Your Spelling and Grammar 13

9 | Use a Menu Bar 14

10 | Sitemaps 15

11 | Provide a "Homepage" Link 16

12 | Provide Site Search 17

13 | Provide Targeted Searches 18

14 | Use Bullet Points 19

15 | Allow Customers to Contact You 20

16 | Copyright Notices 21

17 | Privacy 22

18 | Website Security 23

19 | Money-Back Guarantee 24

20 | Shipping Information 25

21 | Terms of Use 26
22 | Floating Cart 27
23 | Product Photos 28
24 | Sale Prices 29
25 | Free Shipping 30
26 | Whole Numbers 31
27 | MSRP 32
28 | Add to Cart 33
#29 | Inventory Availability 34
30 | Returns Policy 35
31 | Social Media Distractions 36
32 | Landing Pages 37
33 | Breadcrumbs 38
34 | Page Title 39
35 | Item or Part Numbers 40
36 | Product Description 41
37 | Product Specs 42
38 | Shopping Cart 43
39 | Shopping Cart Extras 44
40 | Checkout 45
41 | Credit Cards 46
42 | PayPal® 47
43 | Checkout Extras 48

44 | "Thank You for Your Purchase" Page 50
46 | Order Shipped Email..52
47 | Page Background Color 53
48 | Text Color 54
49 | Link Colors 55
50 | Music, Sound, and Animations................................56
51 | Footers 57
52 | Recently-Viewed Items..58
53 | Related Product Links...59
54 | Order Block Positioning 60
55 | Secondary Order Block 61
56 | Page Width 62
57 | Web Browsers 63
58 | Tablets 64
59 | Smart Phones 65
60 | Focus Groups 66
In Closing..67

www.ingramcontent.com/pod-product-compliance
Lightning Source LLC
Chambersburg PA
CBHW071803170526
45167CB00003B/1156